To

_____

In appreciation for your gift of music

From

_____

Date

_____

MUSIC INFORMATION CENTER
VISUAL & PERFORMING ARTS
CHICAGO PUBLIC LIBRARY

Harold Shaw Publishers
Wheaton, Illinois

© 1999 by Harold Shaw Publishers

Acknowledgments, page 6.

ISBN 0-87788-568-0

Compiled by Mary Horner Collins
Cover and inside design by David LaPlaca

Library of Congress Cataloging-in-Publication Data

Music is your forte : in appreciation of your musical gifts / compiled by Mary Horner Collins.
    p.   cm.
  ISBN 0-87788-568-0 (pbk.)
  1. Music—Quotations, maxims, etc. I. Collins, Mary Horner.
PN6084.M8M87 1999
780—dc21

98-46732
CIP

05 04 03 02 01 00 99

10 9 8 7 6 5 4 3 2 1

To Joanne Maestas,
whose teaching and example
kindled my love for music

Acknowledgments

"Composers' Birthdays–Celebrate!" section is taken from *How to Grow a Young Music Lover: Helping Your Child Discover and Enjoy the World of Music*, ©1994 by Cheri Fuller. Used by permission of Harold Shaw Publishers.

Unless otherwise marked, all Scripture quotations are from the HOLY BIBLE, NEW INTERNATIONAL VERSION ®. NIV ®. Copyright © 1973, 1978, 1984 by International Bible Society. Used by permission of Zondervan Publishing House. All rights reserved. The "NIV" and "New International Version" trademarks are registered in the United States Patent and Trademark Office by International Bible Society. Use of either trademark requires permission of International Bible Society.

Scripture quotations marked THE MESSAGE are from *The Message*. Copyright © 1993, 1994, 1995 by Eugene H. Peterson. Used by permission of NavPress Publishing Group.

Scripture quotations marked NEB are from *The New English Bible*, © The Delegates of Oxford University Press and The Syndics of the Cambridge University Press, 1961. Reprinted with permission.

Scripture quotations marked NKJV are from the New King James Version. Copyright © 1979, 1980, 1982, Thomas Nelson Inc., Publishers.

Scripture quotations marked NLT are taken from the *Holy Bible*, New Living Translation, copyright © 1996. Used by permission of Tyndale House Publishers, Inc., Wheaton, Illinois 60189. All rights reserved.

Scripture quotations marked PHILLIPS are from the Phillips' Translation, *New Testament in Modern English*, rev. ed. by J. B. Phillips. © 1958, 1960, 1972 by J. B. Phillips. Reprinted with permission of the Macmillan Publishing Co., Inc.

Scripture quotations marked RSV are from the Revised Standard Version of the Bible, copyright © 1946, 1952, 1971 by the Division of Christian Education of the National Council of the Churches of Christ in the USA, and are used by permission.

Scriptures marked TEV are taken from *Today's English Version* (The Good News Bible), © 1966, 1971, 1976, 1992 American Bible Society. Used by permission.

What's Inside

Introduction:
For the Love of Music

Mr. Moore, my high school A Cappella choir director, was a gentleman and a class act. He wore a fashionable suit and colorful tie every day. He always spoke formally, calling us "ladies and gentlemen," "Mr. Beck," "Miss Horner." He commanded respect.

But when he directed the choir rehearsals, we saw another side of Mr. Moore. He would take off his jacket, loosen his tie, his face would grimace with every nuance, and at times he would literally run across the room emphasizing a crescendo. He manifested what all great music teachers and directors have: a passion for music and a gift for passing it on.

A love for music, as many other things in life, is caught as well as taught. If you are reading this, then music is probably your forte. You may be a piano teacher, a band director, a church musician, or a choir leader. Whatever your musical role, you have been part of the ongoing chain of musical growth in someone's life. Hence the reason for this little book of reminders about the wonder of music—to thank all the Mr. Moores for enriching our lives.

—Mary Horner Collins

SECTION I

Music's Mystery and Power

There are things that music can do that language can never do, that painting can never do, or sculpture. Music is capable of going directly to the source of the mystery. It doesn't have to explain it. It can simply celebrate it.

—*Marsha Norman*

Among the first things created was the bird. Why? Because God wanted the world to have music at the start. And this infant world, wrapped in swaddling clothes of light, so beautifuly serenaded at the start is to die amid the ringing of the archangel's trumpet; so that as the world had music at the start, it is going to have music at the last.

Thomas De Witt Talmage

Music is a part of us, and either ennobles or degrades our behavior.

Anicius Boethius

We ought to hear at least one little song every day, read a good poem, see a first-rate painting, and if possible speak a few sensible words.

Johann Wolfgang von Goethe

Blessed art Thou, O Lord, who hast revealed thyself in music, and granted me the love of it.

The Contemporary Hebrew

God is its author, and not man; he laid the keynote of all harmonies; he planned all perfect combinations, and he made us so that we could hear and understand.

Anonymous

In a word, [music] is so powerful a thing that it rav-isheth the soul, the queen of the senses, by sweet pleasure. . . . And 'tis not only men that are affected, . . . All singing birds are much pleased with it, especially nightingales . . . and bees among the rest, though they be flying away, when they hear any tingling sound, will tarry behind. Harts, hinds, horses, dogs, bears are ex-ceedingly delighted with it, . . . and in Lydia in the midst of a lake there be certain floating islands (if ye will believe it) that after music will dance.

Robert Burton

[Music is] a form of remembering, a return to the sea-sons of the heart, long ago.

Menotti

Music brings a richness to our experience—a wonder, joy, and beauty that nothing else can. . . . Our spirits can be lifted, our perspectives heightened, our emotions comforted or cheered—all because of an instrumental piece, a hymn, or a song that touches us at several levels.

Cheri Fuller, How to Grow a Young Music Lover

Music, the greatest good that mortals know,
And all of heaven we have below.

Joseph Addison

The drive to express poetic and pictorial thoughts is the essence of music. Music is an invitation to the creative imagination of the hearer to make alive the feelings and the visions from which it derived.

Albert Schweitzer

So is music an asylum. It takes us out of the actual and whispers to us dim secrets that startle our wonder as to who we are, and for what, whence, and whereto, all the great interrogatories, like questioning angels, float in on its waves of sound.

Ralph Waldo Emerson

Such sweet compulsion doth in music lie.

John Milton

Music is the art of the prophets, the only art that can calm the agitations of the soul; it is one of the most magnificent and delightful presents God has given us.

Martin Luther

Music is the only language in which you cannot say a mean or sarcastic thing.

John Erskine

The thought of the eternal efflorescence of music is a comforting one, and comes like a messenger of peace in the midst of universal disturbance.

Romain Rolland

Deeply moving as the words of many of the "spirituals" are, as utterances of the depths of human suffering and sorrow, their great power lies in their music. Almost without exception the melodies possess dignity in their simplicity and breathe the spirit of a deep religious experience.

Henry Wilder Foote, from Three Centuries of American Hymnody

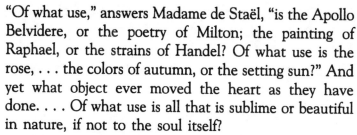

"Of what use," answers Madame de Staël, "is the Apollo Belvidere, or the poetry of Milton; the painting of Raphael, or the strains of Handel? Of what use is the rose, . . . the colors of autumn, or the setting sun?" And yet what object ever moved the heart as they have done. . . . Of what use is all that is sublime or beautiful in nature, if not to the soul itself?

Sir Archibald Allison

I wish to see all arts, principally music, in the service of Him who gave and created them. Music is a fair and

glorious gift of God. I would not for the world forego my humble share of music. Singers are never sorrowful, but are merry, and smile through their troubles in song. Music makes people kinder, gentler, more staid and reasonable.

Martin Luther

Are you hurting? Pray. Do you feel great? Sing.

James 5:13 (THE MESSAGE)

Many a stoic soul, doubtful of the creed, was melted by the music, and fell on his knees before the mystery that no words could speak.

Will Durant, The Age of Faith

The human soul is a silent harp in God's choir whose strings need only to be swept by the divine breath to chime in with the harmonies of creation.

Henry David Thoreau

Perhaps it is only the artists who have not forgotten the cloud of brilliance which shines through all Scripture. . . .

When the priests came out of the sanctuary, the cloud filled the temple of the Lord, and the priests could not bear to minister because of the cloud, for the glory of the Creator of the Galaxies had filled the house of the Lord. . . .

To be an artist means to approach the light, and that means to let go our control, to allow our whole selves to be placed with absolute faith in that which is greater than we are.

Madeleine L'Engle, Walking on Water

O yes! the ascending from out of unconscious life into revelation, that is music!

Bettina von Arnim

[Psalm 150] exhorts us to confess ourselves to God in the cithara as we sing psalms with the ten-string harp; desiring to restore ourselves, let sound the psalterium which gives back the sound from the heavenly realm above for expanding the spirit; let sound the ten-string harp for contemplation of the law.

Hildegard of Bingen

Music my rampart, and my only one.

Edna St. Vincent Millay, upon hearing a symphony by Beethoven

I waited patiently for the Lord;
   he inclined to me and heard my cry.
He drew me up from the desolate pit, . . .
   and set my feet upon a rock.
He put a new song in my mouth,
   a song of praise to our God.

Psalm 40:1-3 (RSV)

I am strongly persuaded that after theology there is no art that can be placed on a level with music; for besides theology, music is the only art capable of affording peace and joy of the heart.

Martin Luther

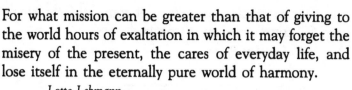

For what mission can be greater than that of giving to the world hours of exaltation in which it may forget the misery of the present, the cares of everyday life, and lose itself in the eternally pure world of harmony.

Lotte Lehmann

The power of music, narrative and drama is one of greatest practical and theoretical importance. . . . We see how the retarded, unable to perform fairly simple tasks involving perhaps four or five movements or procedures in sequence, can do these perfectly if they work to music.

Oliver Sacks, neurologist, The Man Who Mistook His Wife for a Hat

We should comport ourselves with the masterpieces of art as with exalted personages—stand quietly before them and wait till they speak to us.

Arthur Schopenhauer

The wonderful thing about music is that it immediately evokes certain eras of one's life, brings you back to where you've been, even if you don't want to go there.

Donna Matteo, from Interviews with Contemporary Women Playwrights

[Mrs. Elton speaking to Miss Woodhouse]: "To be quite honest, I do not think I can live without something of a musical society. I condition for nothing else, but without music, life would be a blank to me."

Jane Austen, Emma

After silence that which comes nearest to expressing the inexpressible is music.

Aldous Huxley

Music does not exist in a vacuum. It does not exist until it is performed. . . . The magic comes only with the sounding of the music, with the turning of the written notes into sound.

Benjamin Britten, from The Saturday Review *magazine*

O burning Mountain, O chosen Sun,
  O perfect Moon, O fathomless Well.
O unattainable Height, O clearness beyond measure,
  O Wisdom without end, O Mercy without limit,
  O Strength beyond resistance, O Crown beyond all
    majesty;
  The humblest thing you created sings your praise.
  Amen.

Mechtild of Magdeburg

If you like music, you have to love all kinds of music. Which also should go the other way. All those young kids who love pop music should also like classical.

Jean-Yves Thibaudet, from the Los Angeles Times

Music produces a kind of pleasure which human nature cannot do without.

Confucius

There can be no mischief sure where there is music.

Cervantes

After playing Chopin, I feel as if I had been weeping over sins that I had never committed, and mourning over tragedies that were not my own. Music always seems to me to produce that effect. It creates for one a past of which one has been ignorant and fills one with a sense of sorrows that have been hidden from one's tears.

Oscar Wilde

When people hear good music, it makes them homesick for something they never had, and never will have.

E. W. Howey

The only time that our blessed Lord ever is recorded as having sung is the night that he went out to his death.

Fulton J. Sheen

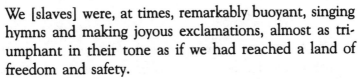

We [slaves] were, at times, remarkably buoyant, singing hymns and making joyous exclamations, almost as triumphant in their tone as if we had reached a land of freedom and safety.

Frederick Douglass, My Bondage and My Freedom

These people had no choir and no organ. They used the drum, the cymbal, the tambourine and the steel triangle. Everybody in there sang, and they clapped and stomped their feet, and sang with their whole bodies. They had a beat, a rhythm we held on to from slavery days, and their music was so strong and expressive. It used to bring tears to my eyes.

Mahalia Jackson, recalling her childhood church

Music and art are a whole spiritual world in Russia. . . . When people go to a concert, they don't go to it as an attraction, as an entertainment, but to feel life.

Mstislav Rostropovich, from the New York Times *magazine*

Thou [music] speakest to me of things which in all my endless life I have not found and shall not find.

Jean Paul Richter

Music is the one form of expression known to humans which is understood by every tribe and nation. . . . thus, to say that music speaks is not an exaggeration for music speaks to the soul of a man. Since this is the case, we should be very particular in our church music for we are not merely entertaining but speaking to the souls of men and women and therfore should be very careful what we "say."

Kenneth Morris

The man that hath no music in himself,
Nor is not mov'd with concord of sweet sounds,
Is fit for treasons, strategems, and spoils;
The motions of his spirit are dull as night,
And his affections dark as Erebus:
Let no such man be trusted.

William Shakespeare, The Merchant of Venice

The hours when the mind is absorbed by beauty are the only hours when we really live, so that the longer we can stay among these things so much the more is snatched from inevitable Time.

Richard Jefferies

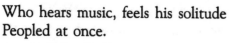

Who hears music, feels his solitude
Peopled at once.

Robert Browning

Whenever the spirit from God came upon Saul, David would take his harp and play. Then relief would come to Saul; he would feel better, and the evil spirit would leave him.

1 Samuel 16:23

[Music]—that real moonlight in every gloomy night of life.

Jean Paul Richter

For the Lord your God has arrived to live among you. He is a mighty savior. He will rejoice over you with great gladness. With his love, he will calm all your fears. He will exult over you by singing a happy song.

Zephaniah 3:17 (NLT)

Music is well said to be the speech of angels; in fact, nothing among the utterances allowed to man is felt to be so divine. It brings us near to the Infinite.

Thomas Carlyle

Take a music-bath once or twice a week for a few seasons, and you will find that it is to the soul what the water-bath is the body.

Oliver Wendell Holmes

Play Mozart in memory of me.

Last words of Frédéric Chopin

If a thing isn't worth saying, you sing it.

Beaumarchais

Without music, life would be an error. The German imagines even God singing songs.

Friedrich Nietzsche

Music and religion are as intimately related as poetry and love; the deepest emotions require for their civilized expression the most emotional of arts.

> *Will Durant*

It is good to praise the Lord
   and make music to your name,
O Most High.

> *Psalm 92:1*

Whether the angels play only Bach in praising God I am not quite sure; I am sure, however, that *en famille* they play Mozart.

> *Karl Barth, quoted in his obituary*

After they had been severely flogged, [Paul and Silas] were thrown into prison. . . . About midnight Paul and Silas were praying and singing hymns to God, and the other prisoners were listening to them.

> *Acts 16:23-25*

Then I heard every creature in heaven and on earth and under the earth and on the sea, and all that is in them, singing:
  "To him who sits on the throne
    and to the Lamb
  be praise and honor and glory
    and power,
  for ever and ever!"
    Revelation 5:13

Music gives wings to the mind, flight to the imagination, a charm to sadness, gaiety and life to everything.
    Plato

To learn whether you are enjoying a piece of music or not you must see whether you find yourself looking at the advertisements of Pears' soap at the end of the libretto.

Samuel Butler

Nothing soothes me more after a long and maddening course of pianoforte recitals than to sit and have my teeth drilled.

George Bernard Shaw

Classic music is the kind that we keep thinking will turn into a tune.

Kin Hubbard

Music with dinner is an insult both to the cook and violinist.

G. K. Chesterton

We often feel sad in the presence of music without words; and often more than that in the presence of music without music.

Mark Twain

Of all the noises I think music the least disagreeable.
> *Samuel Johnson*

Music hath charms to soothe a savage breast,
To soften rocks, or bend a knotted oak.
> *William Congreve*, The Mourning Bride

Music hath "charms to soothe a savage"; this may be so, but I would rather try a revolver on him first.
> *Josh Billings*

Berlioz says nothing in his music, but he says it magnificently.
> *James G. Huneker*

Wagner has beautiful moments, but awful quarter hours.
> *Gioacchino Rossini*

On Talents and Gifts

Insist on yourself; never imitate. Your own gift you can present every moment with the cumulative force of a whole life's cultivation; but of the adopted talent of another you have only an extemporaneous half possession.

—*Ralph Waldo Emerson*

Talent is God-given; be thankful.
Conceit is self-given; be careful.
Thomas La Mance

Just as appetite comes by eating, so work brings inspiration, if inspiration is not discernible at the beginning.
Igor Stravinsky

The simple is not easy.
William Schuman

If people knew how hard I have to work to gain my mastery, it would not seem wonderful at all.
Michelangelo Buonarroti

Women have been too much taken up with helping and encouraging men to place a proper value on their own talent, which they are prone to underestimate and to think not worth making the most of. . . . Ruskin was quite right when he so patronizingly said that "Woman's chief function is praise." She has praised and praised, and kept herself in abeyance. But now, . . . women are beginning to realize that they, too, have brains, and even musical ones.

Amy Fay, 19th century pianist, Music Study in Germany

Exercise, exercise your powers; what is now difficult will finally become routine.

G. C. Lichtenberg

No man who is occupied in doing a very difficult thing, and doing it very well, ever loses his self-respect.

George Bernard Shaw

The conductor is much more like a general than a mother or teacher. It's a kind of enforced leadership, the kind more likely to be expected of men than women. A woman conductor, because of these traditions, must rely completely on being able to transmit authority purely on the grounds of her musical ability.

Victoria Bond, from Women at Work

It is one thing to praise discipline, and another to submit to it.

Cervantes

[On what he looks for in a chorus singer]: I look for voice, of course, a blendable voice. I look for musicality. It's also a matter of personality; a chorister has to have patience, discipline, a strong sense of self-worth. Working in a collective situation requires a certain kind of balanced temperament, a sense of being happy with oneself.

Raymond Hughes, from Opera News *magazine*

An ounce of work is worth many pounds of words.

St. Francis de Sales

One must work, nothing but work. And one must have patience.

Auguste Rodin

I do not like work even when another person does it.

Mark Twain

What we call "creative work" ought not to be called work at all, because it isn't. . . . I imagine Thomas Edison never did a day's work in his last fifty years.

Stephen Leacock

I never sing songs I don't like. . . . If there's not a sense of timelessness, I don't go near it.

Tony Bennett, from USA Today

Anyone can do any amount of work, provided it isn't the work he is *supposed* to be doing at the moment.

Robert Benchley

The body is truly the garment of the soul, which has a living voice; for that reason it is fitting that the body simultaneously with the soul repeatedly sing praises to God through the voice.

Hildegard of Bingen

A man must not deny his manifest abilities, for that is to evade his obligations.

Robert Louis Stevenson

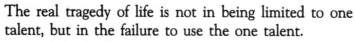

Stewards are expected to show themselves trustworthy. . . . What do you possess that was not given you? If then you really received it all as a gift, why take the credit to yourself?

St. Paul, 1 Corinthians 4:2-7 (NEB)

The real tragedy of life is not in being limited to one talent, but in the failure to use the one talent.

Edgar W. Work

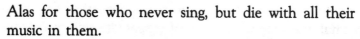

Alas for those who never sing, but die with all their music in them.

Oliver Wendell Holmes

[Mrs. Elton speaking to Miss Woodhouse]: "I think you and I must establish a musical club and have regular weekly meetings at your house or ours. Will it not be a good plan? If *we* exert ourselves, I think we shall not be long in want of allies. Something of that nature would be particularly desirable for *me* as an inducement to keep me in practice; for married women, you know—there is a sad story against them, in general. They are but too apt to give up music."

Jane Austen, Emma

Next to excellence is the appreciation of it.

William Makepeace Thackeray

Praise the Lord with the harp;
   make music to him on the
      ten-stringed lyre.
Sing to him a new song;
   play skillfully, and shout for joy.

King David, Psalm 33:2-3

The world is always ready to receive talent with open arms. Very often it does not know what to do with genius.

Oliver Wendell Holmes

I heard Clara Schumann on Sunday. . . . She seems to throw herself into the music, instead of letting the music take possession of her. She gives you the most exquisite pleasure with every note she touches. . . . . She seemed full of fire, and when she played Bach, she ought to have been crowned with diamonds! Such noble playing I never heard.

Amy Fay, Music Study in Germany

Lord, grant that I may always desire more than I can accomplish.

Michelangelo Buonarroti

I know what these people want; I have seen them pick up my violin and turn it over in their hands. They may not know it themselves, but they want music, not by the ticketful, the purseful, but music as it should be had, music at home, a part of daily life, a thing as necessary, as satisfying, as the midday meal. They want to *play*. And they are kept back by the absurd, the mistaken, the wicked notion that in order to play an instrument one must be possessed by that bogey called Talent.

Catherine Drinker Bowen, *from* Friends and Fiddlers

God save me from a bad neighbor and a beginner on the fiddle.

Italian Proverb

Doing easily what others find difficult is talent; doing what is impossible is genius.

Henri Frédérick Amiel

No one respects a talent that is concealed.

Desiderius Erasmus

No talent can survive the blight of neglect.

Edgar A. Whitney

Music is . . . playing your own tune while keeping time with the rest of the band.

Unknown

[Our] separation has once more made me very conscious of my peculiar and difficult position. Am I to neglect my own talent, in order to serve you as companion on your journeys? Have you allowed your talent to lie useless, or ought you to do so, because I am chained to the paper and to the piano? Now, when you are so young and in full possession of your powers? We found the solution. You took a companion with you, and I came back to the child and my work. But what will the world say? . . . Yet it is necessary that we should find some means by which we can both utilise and develop our talents side by side.

Robert Schumann, to his wife Clara

So whether you eat or drink or whatever you do, do it all for the glory of God.

St. Paul, 1 Corinthians 10:31

Never to tire, never to grow cold; to be patient, sympathetic, tender; to look for the budding flower and the

40

opening heart; to hope always, like God, to love always—this is duty.

Henri Frédérick Amiel

I never pretended to have a great voice. It works and I can carry a tune. If you have a good song, that's about all that's required.

Willie Nelson, from the New York Times

When your work speaks for itself, don't interrupt.

Henry Kaiser

You carry with you all your experiences on stage and you build on that. Each performance is a rehearsal for the next one. Whatever I play in public I like, and if I learn something, it's not to play for this week or that week, but forever.

Van Cliburn, from the Los Angeles Times

The greatest secret of good work whether in music, literature or art lies in not attempting too much; if it is

asked, "What is too much?" the answer is, "Anything that we find difficult or unpleasant."

Samuel Butler

So much unhappiness, it seems to me, is due to nerves; and bad nerves are the result of having nothing to do, or doing a thing badly, unsuccessfully or incompetently. Of all the unhappy people in the world, the unhappiest are those who have not found something they want to do. True happiness comes to him who does his work well, followed by a relaxing and refreshing period of rest. True happiness comes from the right amount of work for the day.

Lin Yutang

Beethoven can write music, thank God,
but he can do nothing else on earth.

Ludwig van Beethoven, in a letter to Ferdinand Reis

If you would have your lamp burn, pour oil into it.

German Proverb

Because kind Nature had endowed [Handel] with genius, he did not throw himself with the less ardour into the study of counterpoint.

W. S. Rockstro, The Life of G. F. Handel

Do what you can, with what you have, where you are.

Theodore Roosevelt

Even though I felt it myself, I sometimes doubted whether it was only for a woman, and an Englishwoman living in a not musical circle, that I was anything particular in music—whether such talent as I have deserved to have everything else put aside for it. And now I know it does deserve it! The greatest musical genius I know [Henschel] has seen my work and so to speak has given it his blessing, and it is well with me!

Ethel Smythe, early 20th century composer

Every good gift and every perfect present comes from heaven; it comes down from God.

James the apostle, James 1:17 (TEV)

Every day that is born into this world comes like a burst of music, . . . and thou shalt make of it a dance, a dirge, or a life march, as thou wilt.

Thomas Carlyle

Music is a demanding enterprise; you must do it with love—or not at all.

John Bowles

It's a pity to shoot the pianist when the piano is out of tune.

René Coty

Miss [Margaret] Truman is a unique American phenomenon with a pleasant voice of little size and fair quality. . . . There are few moments during her recital when one can relax and feel confident that she will make her goal, which is the end of the song.

Paul Hume

If a thing is worth doing, it is worth doing badly.

G. K. Chesterton

Difficult—I wish it had been impossible.

Samuel Johnson, after a violinist had exhibited his virtuosity

She was a singer who had to take any note above A with her eyebrows.

Montague Glass

On a Lighter Note

A young woman whose voice had been gradually deteriorating over the years replied, in answer to my enquiry as to her progress, "Madame is delighted with me. She tells me that I have great potentiality, that my voice is like a large mansion with many gorgeous salons and chambers, but at present these rooms are closed and shuttered. At the moment, Madame says, I am merely in the entresol of this mansion, and in two or three years all these wonderful rooms will be opened if I continue to take my lessons with her regularly.

Gerald Moore, preface to The Singer and His Art, *by Aksel Schitz*

Passing the Gift On

How indeed does anyone describe adequately what is learned from a powerful teacher? I myself have never read a convincing account of the progress from student stage to that of creative maturity through a teacher's ministrations. And yet it happens: some kind of magic does indubitably rub off on the pupil.

—*Aaron Copland*

The trouble with music appreciation in general is that people are taught to have too much respect for music; they should be taught to love it instead.

Igor Stravinsky, from the New York Times *magazine*

Teaching others, we learn ourselves.

Sen. Epistolae

To find out what one is fitted to do and to secure an opportunity to do it is the key to happiness.

John Dewey

I think that [being musical is] something you either have or you don't. It's not something you learn. I think there are people who feel the highs and lows of music well, but can get lost during the rest. And there are those who are more mathematical and can be with the music, but they don't *feel* it; they're just doing the correct thing. And then there are those who are musical, who hear the music and feel it.

Joanna Berman, Dance *magazine*

A Tutor who tooted the flute
Tried to teach two young tutors to toot;
  Said the two to the Tutor,
  "Is it harder to toot, or
To tutor two tutors to toot?"
     Carolyn Wells

It is a fine thing to have ability, but the ability to discover ability in others is the true test.
     Elbert Kipling

A bad teacher can ruin a voice. Is this young person forcing in the upper register, trying to turn herself into a lyric soprano when in reality she is a mezzo? . . . Only a pedagogue with knowledge and experience can supply [the answer]. He must assess the possibilities of the pupil's voice, tend it, place it, guard it from injurious habits.
     Aksel Schitz, The Singer and His Art

By a process of osmosis one soaks up [the teacher's] attitudes, principles, reflections, knowledge. That last is

49

a key word: it is literally exhilarating to be with a
teacher for whom the art one loves has no secrets.

Aaron Copland, from Harper's *magazine*

We must not only give what we *have*; we must also give
what we *are*.

Désiré Joseph Mercier

When'er you lecture, be concise: the soul
Takes in short maxims, and retains them whole;
But pour in water when the vessel's filled,
It simply dribbles over and is spilled.

Horatius

Patience! patience! though heart should break.

Lenore Bürger

So many of the young singers are singing music they
can cope with musically, but they have not worked on
their technique sufficiently to be in command of what
their voices are doing. . . . Some of the younger singers

seem to have in their minds what the music is, but they don't actually sing it. And they think they are singing it! I don't know how they can do that, nor do I know how their teachers let them get away with the inaccuracy of pitch and the lack of correctness.

Joan Sutherland, from Opera News *magazine*

An orchestra is like a living organism. It needs to be in touch with its progenitors. . . . Youth has to study with somebody.

Yuri Temirkanov, from the Los Angeles Times

Polyxena Fletcher had genius. . . . Music life and people were inseparable to her, and our lessons, which lasted hours and seemed timeless, were occupied as much with talk and discussion as piano playing.

Elisabeth Lutyens, 20th century composer, A Goldfish Bowl

We can assert with confidence that without Haydn we should not have the Mozart we know; that without Mozart we should not have the Beethoven we know;

and that without Beethoven the whole musical history of the nineteenth century would have been utterly different from what it is.

A. J. Balfour, Essays and Addresses

Listen to music religiously, as if it were the last strain you might hear.

Henry David Thoreau

It's more important to play the wrong note right than the right note wrong.

Artur Rubenstein, from High Fidelity magazine

What I [as a singing teacher] am asking people to do is stand there and take all the armor off. . . . Safety lies in the thing that seems most dangerous—letting people see your emotional stuff. . . . When I hear a singer who allows me to come in emotionally, they've got me. Because the most fascinating thing on earth to people is another person.

Barbara Cook, from Opera News magazine

To please, one must make up his mind to be taught many things which he already knows, by people who do not know them.

    Nicholas Chamfort

Personally, I am always ready to learn, although I do not always like being taught.

    Winston Churchill

No doubt, if women music teachers could get plenty of pupils, they would be able to teach them; but here is precisely the difficulty. . . . A woman is at a disadvantage on account of her sex, and the reason of this is that, as a rule, boys and young men do not study music. Young girls find it more interesting to take of a man teacher, and this would be alright if the young men would return the compliment.

    Amy Fay, 19th century pianist, "The Woman Teacher in a Large City"

Music helps the child to discover beauty. Children's eyes are very sensitive to bright and beautiful colors. We should also develop their sensitivity to beautiful musical sounds.

Unknown

Just as there can be no music without learning, no education is complete without music. Music makes the difference.

Unknown

We are expected to dance at weddings, cheer at sporting events while clapping hands in time with the crowd, sing "Happy Birthday" to friends and relatives, or share a lullaby with an infant. . . . Regardless of our ultimate level of involvement with music, the success of our musical experiences may depend on the musical nurturing we received during our preschool years.

Music Educator's Journal, *January 1991*

A musicologist is a man who can read music but can't hear it.

Sir Thomas Beecham

A good teacher is one whose ears get as much exercise as his mouth.

Proverb

Teachers open the door. You enter by yourself.

Chinese Proverb

At the Berkeley Symphony, democracy is not just a word. If a passage is slow in coming together, ranting and raving won't help. I need to work with the orchestra toward a constructive solution. We have to remember that our job is not to serve ourselves, it's to serve music and our community.

Ken Nagano, from Harper's magazine

We too often get bound to the printed page and stick with that alone. But Mozart must have been a wildly

expressive person. He used to yell and scream at rehearsals, not about technical perfection but about expression. As a conductor, this is where my instinct and insight come in. I think of what expression is there, and how it sings.

Vincent la Selva, from Opera News *magazine*

I do everything from the heart, from personal conviction. If you try to find love by charting a course, you'll never find it.

Van Cliburn, from the New York Times

It's too bad that one of the first things to go in our schools is the art programs. . . . When there's an economic situation, music, dance, theater and visual arts are the first things to be cut, while sports gets all the attention and money. Sports are certainly important, but we stress them so much at the expense of art, leaving out young people who don't have the physical strength for sports, or the interest. After all, civilizations are remembered because of their art.

Jacob Lawrence, from Booklist *magazine*

The arts have to be a continuing effort, a fight for the minds and the freedom of our children, and not just social adornment.

Isaac Stern, the New York Times

Experience teaches us much, but learns us little.

Josh Billings

The object of teaching a child is to enable him to get along without a teacher.

Elbert Hubbard

Training is everything: the peach was once a bitter almond; cauliflower is nothing but cabbage with a college education.

Mark Twain

[Liszt] gives *no* paid lessons whatever, as he is much too grand for that, but if one has talent enough, or pleases him, he lets one come to him and play to him. . . . Nothing could exceed Liszt's amiability, or the trouble he gave himself, and instead of frightening me, he inspired me. Never was there such a delightful teacher! and he is the first sympathetic one I've had. You feel so *free* with him, and he develops the very spirit of music in you. He doesn't keep nagging at you all the time, but he leaves you your own conception. Now and then he will make a criticism, or play a passage, and with a few words give you enough to think of all the rest of your life.

Amy Fay, Music Study in Germany

Teachers are the hours who open or close the gates of heaven.

Jean Paul Richter

The teacher is like the candle that lights others in consuming itself.

Italian Proverb

I'm a musician who hopes to be inspired enough to inspire others, to be somewhere along the chain of influences that encourages constructive values like passion, sensitivity and joy to emerge from music.

Herbie Hancock, from DownBeat *magazine*

You cannot teach a man anything; you can only help him to find it himself.

Galileo Galilei

No horse gets anywhere until he is harnessed. No steam or gas ever drives anything until it is confined. No Niagara is ever turned into light and power until it is tunneled. No life ever grows great until it is focused, dedicated, disciplined.

Harry Emerson Fosdick

No teacher should strive to make men think as he thinks, but to lead them to the living Truth, to the Master himself, of whom alone they can learn anything.

George MacDonald

Musical training is a more potent instrument than any other, because rhythm and harmony find their way into the inward places of the soul.

Plato

It is in learning music that many youthful hearts learn to love.

Ricard

The Music Makers

We are the music-makers
And we are the dreamers of dreams,
Wandering by lonely sea breakers,
And sitting by desolate streams;
World-losers and world-forsakers,
On whom the pale moonlight gleams:
Yet we are the movers and shakers
Of the world forever, it seems.
—*Arthur O'Shaughnessy, "Ode"*

What is to reach the heart must come from above; if it does not come from thence, it will be nothing but notes, body without spirit.

Ludwig van Beethoven

I should be sorry, my lord, [Lord Kinnoull] if I have only succeeded in entertaining them; I wished to make them better.

George Frederick Handel, following the first performance of Messiah *in London*

It is the best of all trades, to make songs, and the second best to sing them.

Hilaire Belloc

God is the greatest of all composers, who has composed the universe of universes.

Karl Stockhausen, from Trackings *by R. Dufallo*

Art is a collaboration between God and the artist, and the less the artist does the better.

André Gide

All real works of art look as if they were done in joy.

Robert Henri

I have to play to people for a few pretty words and a cup of warm water, and get home, dead tired, at 11 or 12 o'clock, drink a draught of water, lie down, and think, "Is an artist much more than a beggar?" And yet art is a fine gift! What, indeed, is finer to clothe one's feelings in music, what a comfort in time of trouble, what a pleaure, what an exquisite feeling, to give happy hours to so many people by its means. And what an exalted feeling so to follow art that one gives one's life to it!

Clara Schumann, in a letter to Robert Schumann

The aim of art is to represent not the outward appearance of things, but their inward significance.

Aristotle

To be an artist is a great thing, but to be an artist and not know it is the most glorious plight in the world.

James M. Barrie

Art is the signature of man.

G. K. Chesterton

In the beginning God created the heavens and the earth. . . . God saw all that he had made, and it was very good.

Genesis 1:1-31

[God's creative song] ordered the universe concordantly and tuned the discord of the elements in an harmonious arrangement, so that the entire cosmos might become through its agency a consonance.

Clement of Alexandria

A necessary part of [Jesus'] command to love is that we should live with integrity and seek the truth: love cannot develop without this. It follows that creative artists must have this goal not just for their life but also for their work.

Andrew Wilson-Dickson, The Story of Christian Music

Art is the gift of God and must be used for his glory.

Henry Wadsworth Longfellow

For Bach, all music was religion; writing it was an act of faith, and performing it was an act of worship. Every note was dedicated to God and to nothing else. And this was true of all his music, no matter how secular its purpose.

Leonard Bernstein, The Joy of Music

[Psalm 150] orders that God be praised with cymbals of jubilation and with the rest of the musical instruments which the wise and studious have created, since all of the arts (whose purpose is to fill uses and needs of man) are brought to life by that breath of life which God breathed into the body of man: and therefore it is just that God be praised in all things.

Hildegard of Bingen

All great art is the expression of man's delight in God's work, not his own.

John Ruskin

Art and religion go together perfectly; both spiral out from the familiar, both aspire to the boundless.

Jonathan Harvey, from the Musical Times *magazine*

Art is the telling of truth and is the only available method for telling of certain truths.

Iris Murdoch

The idea that there is a truth to be sought in art was well known in earlier times when the musics of cosmos, human soul, and voice were assumed to be in subtle synchrony. But truth in art is still a reality.

Andrew Wilson-Dickson, The Story of Christian Music

Art is the right hand of nature. The latter has only given us being; the former has made us men.

Johann C. F. von Schiller

I do not play the guitar for applause. I sing the difference that there is between what is true and what is false; otherwise I do not sing.

Violeta Parra

A painter paints his pictures on canvas. But musicians paint their pictures in silence. We provide the music and you [the audience] provide the silence.

Leopold Stokowski

A good spectator also creates.

Swiss Proverb

True composition is inexplicable. No one can explain how the notes of a Mozart melody, or the folds of a piece of Titian's drapery, produce their essential effects on each other. If you do not feel it, no one can by reasoning make you feel it.

John Ruskin

On the writing down of the first sound I become totally obsessed until the work is finished; compressing in a short time the number of hours some composers spread over months. Afterwards I have little interest in the work beyond assessing from the first performance to what extent I have succeeded in achieving what I intended. (Luckily, I love my children—after birth!)

Elisabeth Lutyens, A Goldfish Bowl

Nevertheless, the passions, whether violent or not, should never be so expressed as to reach the point of causing disgust; and music, even in situations of the greatest horror, should never be painful to the ear but should flatter and charm it, and thereby always remain music.

Wolfgang Amadeus Mozart

Art consists in the faithful reflection of the artist's personality.

Unknown

[In composing and arranging music,] you start with a blank page, . . . you start out with nothing there, . . . and the process is the most beautiful part. You know, there are two kinds of composers: one who sees the goal across the park and just runs straight to it; and the other who goes to the park, stops, takes a leaf and feels it, takes his shoes off, and puts his feet in the water for a while. You're going across the park anyway, so you might as well take the trip.

Quincy Jones, from Interview *magazine*

We enjoy lovely music, beautiful paintings, a thousand intellectual delicacies, but we have no idea of their cost to those who invented them, in sleepless nights, tears, spasmodic laughter, rashes, asthmas, epilepsies, and the fear of death.

Marcel Proust

I take from European music what I find good in it and use it. As rice is different from beans, so is African music

different from European music. . . . If any of them can be called superior, I think it is the product of the mixture.

Ikoli Harcourt Whyte, Nigerian composer

[Elisabeth-Claude Jacquet de la Guerre (1664–1727)] had a very great genius for composition and excelled in vocal Music the same as in instrumental. . . . One can say that never had a person of her sex had such talents as she for the composition of music, and for the admirable manner in which she performed it at the Harpsichord and on the Organ.

Carol Neuls-Bates, from Women in Music

Composing a piece of music is very feminine. It is sensitive, emotional, contemplative. By comparison, doing housework is positively masculine.

Barbara Kolb, from Time *magazine*

[Women] are, at last, studying composition seriously, and will, ere long, feel out a path for themselves, instead of being "mere imitators of men." . . . Men have been imitators of each other at first. We all know that Mozart began to write like Haydn, and Beethoven began to write like Mozart, before each developed his own originality of style. . . . Why, then, should we expect of women what men could not do? If it has required 50,000 years to produce a male Beethoven, surely one little century ought to be vouchsafed to create a female one!

Amy Fay, 19th century pianist, Music Study in Germany

To me, [sincerity in the music] is the goal. Art is sincere. Somehow you can tell the difference when a song is written just to get on the radio and when what someone does is their whole life. That comes through in Bob Dylan, Paul Simon, Willie Nelson. There is no separating their life from their music. The craft of it becomes their life, too.

Lyle Lovett, from the Los Angeles Times

Jazz is like a good conversation: You have to listen to what others [in the group] have to say [musically] if you're going to make an intelligent contribution.

Wynton Marsalis, from DownBeat *magazine*

To listen is an effort, and just to hear is no merit. A duck hears also.

Igor Stravinsky

A musical experience needs three human beings at least; it requires a composer, a performer, and a listener. . . . Music demands . . . as much effort on the listener's part as the two other corners of the the triangle: *this holy triangle* of composer, performer, and listener.

Benjamin Britten, from the Saturday Review *magazine*

The conductor is a kind of sculptor whose element is time instead of marble.

Leonard Bernstein, The Joy of Music

There are times . . . when a constellation of artists working on [an opera] is all one could wish for; and then there are certain times when it isn't. . . . In reality, people arrive at the rehearsal period and interact with one another based on chemistry, on where they are in their own technical and interpretive developments, and at various stages in their growth in life.

James Levine, from Opera News *magazine*

New artists must break a hole in the subconscious and go fishing there.

Robert Beverly Hale, from Time *magazine*

The notes I handle no better than many pianists. But the pauses between the notes—ah, that is where the art resides!

Artur Schnabel, from Chicago Daily News

A nation creates music—the composer only arranges it.

Mikhail Glinka, from Theatre Arts *magazine*

A lot of us assume, when we hear a symphony today, that it must have spilled out of Beethoven in one steady gush. . . . But not at all. Beethoven left pages and pages of discarded material. . . . The man rejected, rewrote, scratched out, tore up, and sometimes altered a passage as many as twenty times.

Leonard Bernstein, The Joy of Music

Bach was not aware of the uniqueness and greatness of his work. . . . He stands perhaps highest among creative artists. His creative energies expressed themselves without self-consciousness.

Albert Schweitzer

There are passages here and there from which connoisseurs alone can derive satisfaction; but these passages are written in such a way that the less learned cannot fail to be pleased, though without knowing why.

Wolfgang Amadeus Mozart, letter to his father about a concerto he was composing

Divine fires do not blaze each day, but an artist functions in their afterglow hoping for their recurrence.

Ned Rorem, Music from Inside Out

Sing among yourselves psalms and hymns and spiritual songs, your voices making music in your hearts for the ears of the Lord!

St. Paul, Ephesians 5:19 (PHILLIPS)

Just as the body of Christ was born of the Holy Spirit, . . . just so is the song of praise according to the heavenly music radiated by the Holy Spirit in the Church. The body is truly a garment of the soul, which has a living voice; for that reason it is fitting that the body simultaneously with the soul repeatedly sing praises to God through the voice.

Hildegard of Bingen

In order to compose, all you need to do is remember a tune that nobody else has thought of.

Robert Schumann

Somebody once asked Anton Bruckner:

"Master, how, when, where did you think of the divine motif of your Ninth Symphony?"

"Well, it was like this. I walked up the Kahlenberg, and when it got hot and I got hungry, I sat down by a little brook and unpacked my Swiss cheese. And just as I open the greasy paper, that darn tune pops into my head!"

Peter Altenberg

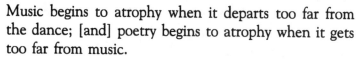

Music begins to atrophy when it departs too far from the dance; [and] poetry begins to atrophy when it gets too far from music.

Ezra Pound

In the future we will have pop song cycles like classical Lieder, but we will create our own words, music, and orchestrations, because we are a generation of whole people.

Judy Collins, from Rock and Other Four Letter Words

My art is contemporary because I live in the present, but also adhere to the belief that one should be inner-directed and that art should reflect its pure source—the soul of its creator.

Robert Haozous, Apache artist

To be faithful, Christian artists should see to it that art and music serve God with all the potential endowed by the Creator. . . . We need popular [Christian] music not just for worship. We need it to celebrate precious moments in life, to open our eyes to injustice, to lighten the load while we work, to energize us while we play.

William Romanowski, from CCM *magazine*

One way of learning art is to choose a master and then try to copy that master; another is to take off on your own and then try to master whoever you are.

Allan Houser

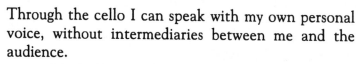

Through the cello I can speak with my own personal voice, without intermediaries between me and the audience.

Mstislav Rostropovich, from Newsweek *magazine*

Bach commands a language of sound. His music is a vehicle of recurring rhythmical motifs, voicing peaceful happiness, living joy, intense pain, or misery sublimely met.

Albert Schweitzer

Music [can] no longer be called a *terra incognita*. When Mozart died, all its great mines, as far as we can see, had at last been opened.

H. R. Haweis, from Music and Morals

Handel was the most incorrigible dreamer, the most irrepressible romanticist, that ever lived; and every note he wrote proves it. But beneath his dreams, there was a fund of practical good sense. . . . We read in old-world stories of dreams which work their own fulfilment. His dreams were of that order.

W. S. Rockstro, Life of G. F. Handel

In Haydn's oratorios, the notes present to the imagination, not only motions, as of the snake, the stag, and the elephant, but colours also; as the green grass. The law of harmonic sounds reappears in the harmonic colours.

Ralph Waldo Emerson

In this [nineteenth century] age of mercenary musical manufacture and art degradation, Mendelssohn towers above his contemporaries like a moral lighthouse in the midst of a dark and troubled sea.

H. R. Haweis, from Music and Morals

For [Bach], art . . . had no concern with the world and success in worldly affairs. It was an end in itself. . . . All great art, even if it is called secular, is really religious

from his point of view. For him the tones do not fade away—they rise as an ineffable praise to God.

Albert Schweitzer

Lord, we know that thou rejoicest
o'er each work of thine;
thou didst ears and hands and voices
for thy praise design:
craftman's art and music's measure,
for thy pleasure all combine.

In thy house, great God, we offer
of thine own to thee,
and for thine acceptance proffer
all unworthily
hearts and minds and hands and voices
in thy choicest psalmody.

Author unknown

Songs of Loudest Praise

Come, thou fount of ev'ry blessing,
Tune my heart to sing thy grace;
Streams of mercy, never ceasing,
Call for songs of loudest praise.

—*Robert Robinson, "Come, Thou Fount
of Every Blessing"*

Music is God's best gift to man, the only art of heaven given to earth, and the only art of earth that we can take to heaven.

Charles Landon

For when we Sing unto God, we ought to sing chearfully, and with loud voice, and heartily to rejoyce. . . . 'Tis Sad to hear what whining, toting, yelling, or Screeking there is in many Country Congregations, as if the people were affrighted, or distracted.

Thomas Nace

I make no pretences to the name of poet or polite writer. . . . I am ambitious to be a servant to the churches and a helper to the joy of the meanest Christian. . . . It was hard to sink every line to the level of a whole congregation, and yet to keep it above [critical] contempt.

Isaac Watts

Tune me, O Lord, into one harmony
With thee, one full responsive vibrant chord;
Unto thy praise, all love and melody,
Tune me, O Lord.

Christina Rossetti

Music is ecstasy, a heart leaping, an explosion of God's joy.

Anonymous

A hymn is a song containing praise of God. If you praise God, but without song, you do not have a hymn. If you praise anything which does not pertain to the glory of God, even if you sing it, you do not have a hymn. Hence a hymn contains the three elements: *song* and *praise* of God.

St. Augustine

Before the leader of church music can attain the art of choosing the right song at the right time, he must know how to select songs of worth and value from which he

may make a choice; then test the songs for religious content, words, literary quality, tune and trust.

Kenneth Morris

I believe we should consider church music basically to be *theological* expression—part of the dialogue between God and worshipers. . . . For this reason, we should choose literature—for instance, hymns and choir pieces—in which the music "fits" the text. True, good words may be supported and enhanced by a variety of musics. But the music, or dance, or any other art, must be the *servant* of theological truth, not the master.

Donald Hustad, True Worship

Teach them to sing by note, and to sing our tunes first: take care they do not sing too slow. Exhort all that can in every congregation to sing. Set them right that sing wrong. Be patient therein.

Methodist Conference, 1765

There is . . . a sense in which all natural agents, even inanimate ones, glorify God continually by revealing the powers he has given them. And in that sense we, as natural agents, do the same. . . . An excellently performed piece of music, as a natural operation which reveals in a very high degree the peculiar powers given to man, will thus always glorify God whatever the intention of the performers may be.

C. S. Lewis

The aim and final reason, as of all music, . . . should be none else but the Glory of God and recreation of the mind. Where this is not observed, there will be no real music but only a devilish hubbub.

J. S. Bach

The devil flees before the sound of music almost as much as before the Word of God.

Martin Luther

Let the sea roar, and all its fullness,
The world and those who dwell in it;
Let the rivers clap their hands;
Let the hills be joyful together
   before the Lord.

Psalm 98:7-8 (NKJV)

God sent His singers upon the earth
With songs of sadness and of mirth,
That they might touch the hearts of men,
And bring them back to heaven again.

Henry Wadsworth Longfellow

While we sing the praises of God in His church, we are
employed in that part of worship which of all others is
the nearest akin to heaven, and 'tis pity that this of all
others should be performed the worst upon earth.

Isaac Watts

God is the organist, we are his instrument,
His Spirit sounds each pipe and gives the tone its strength.

Angelus Silesius

Blues are the songs of despair; gospel songs are the songs of hope.

Mahalia Jackson

He who sings, prays twice.

Attributed to Martin Luther

There are two musical situations on which I think we can be confident that a blessing rests. One is where a priest or an organist, himself a man of trained and delicate taste, humbly and charitably sacrifices his own (esthetically right) desires and gives the people humbler and coarser fare . . . in a belief that he can thus bring them to God. The other is where a stupid and unmusical layman humbly and patiently . . . listens to music which he cannot, or cannot fully, appreciate, in the belief that it somehow glorifies God. . . . To both, Church

Music will have been a means of grace. . . . They have both offered, sacrificed, their taste.

C. S. Lewis, Christian Reflections

A hymn is both poetry and theology, and our culture has little interest in either!

Donald Hustad, True Worship

Music is as well or better able to praise [God] than the building of the church and all its decorations: it is the Church's greatest ornament. . . . Religious music without religion is almost always vulgar.

Igor Stravinsky, from Conversations with Igor Stravinsky

Praise the Lord.
Praise God in his sanctuary;
   praise him in his mighty heavens.
Praise him for his acts of power;
   praise him for his surpassing greatness.
Praise him with the sounding of the trumpet,
   praise him with the harp and lyre,

praise him with tambourine and dancing,
  praise him with the strings and flute,
praise him with the clash of cymbals,
  praise him with resounding cymbals.
Let everything that has breath
  praise the Lord.
Praise the Lord.

Psalm 150

Worship is the highest act of which humans are capable. It not only stretches us beyond all the limits of our finite selves to affirm the divine depth of mystery and holiness in the living and eternal God, but it opens us at the deepest levels of our being to an act that unites us with others.

Samuel H. Miller, adapted

Our music for worship should not be the music we worship.

Donald Hustad, True Worship

And all the Levitical singers, Asaph, Heman, and Jeduthun, their sons and kinsmen, arrayed in fine linen, with cymbals, harps, and lyres, stood east of the altar with a hundred and twenty priests who were trumpeters; and it was the duty of the trumpeters and singers to make themselves heard in unison in praise and thanksgiving to the Lord, and when the song was raised, with trumpets and cymbals and other musical instruments, in praise to the Lord,

"For he is good,

for his steadfast love endures for ever."

2 Chronicles 5:12-13 (RSV)

I heard the voice which comes from the living light bringing forth the different forms of praise, . . . "Praise him in the sound of the trumpet; praise him in the psalterum and cithara" etc., to which was added: "Let every spirit praise the Lord" (Psalm 150). In these words we are instructed about the interior life through exterior things: namely, just how to give form to the Offices serving the interior of human beings and direct them as much as possible towards the praises of the Creator, whether according to the setting of the texts or the nature of the instruments.

Hildegard of Bingen

Let all the world in every corner sing,
"My God and King!"
The heavens are not too high,
His praise may thither fly;
The earth is not too low,
His praises there may grow.
Let all the world in every corner sing,
"My God and King!"

George Herbert, "Hymn"

Composers' Birthdays–Celebrate!

JANUARY
Wolfgang Amadeus Mozart   January 27, 1756
Franz Schubert   January 31, 1797

FEBRUARY
Felix Mendelssohn   February 3, 1809
Arcangelo Corelli   February 17, 1653
George Frederick Handel   February 23, 1685
Jimmy Dorsey   February 29, 1904
Gioacchino Rossini   February 29, 1792

MARCH
Frederic Chopin   March 1, 1810
Glenn Miller   March 1, 1904
Bedrich Smetana   March 2, 1824
Mario Davidovsky   March 4, 1934
Antonio Vivaldi   March 4, 1678
Maurice Ravel   March 7, 1875
C. P. E. Bach   March 8, 1714
Samuel Barber   March 9, 1910
Henry Cowell   March 11, 1897
Nicolay Rimsky-Korsakov   March 18, 1844
Johann Sebastian Bach   March 21, 1685
Modest Mussorgsky   March 21, 1839

Composers' Birthdays–Celebrate!

Béla Bartók	March 25, 1881
Ferde Grofé	March 27, 1892
Paul Whiteman	March 28, 1890
Franz Joseph Haydn	March 31, 1732

APRIL

Sergei Prokofiev	April 23, 1891
Duke Ellington	April 29, 1899

MAY

Lorenz (Larry) Hart	May 2, 1895
Johannes Brahms	May 7, 1833
Peter Ilich Tchaikovsky	May 7, 1840
Irving Berlin	May 11, 1888
Richard Wagner	May 22, 1813
Benny Goodman	May 30, 1909

JUNE

Robert Schumann	June 8, 1810
Frederick Loewe	June 10, 1904
Richard Strauss	June 11, 1864
Edvard Grieg	June 15, 1843
Igor Stravinsky	June 17, 1882
Richard Rodgers	June 28, 1902

Composers' Birthdays–Celebrate!

JULY

Gustav Mahler	July 7, 1860
Oscar Hammerstein	July 12, 1895

AUGUST

Leonard Bernstein	August 15, 1918
Claude Debussy	August 22, 1862
Alan Lerner	August 31, 1918

SEPTEMBER

John Cage	September 5, 1912
Antonin Dvorák	September 8, 1841
Arnold Schönberg	September 13, 1874
Charles Griffes	September 17, 1884
Dimitri Shostakovich	September 25, 1906
George Gershwin	September 26, 1898

OCTOBER

Steve Reich	October 3, 1936
Camille Saint-Saëns	October 9, 1835
Giuseppe Verdi	October 9 or 10, 1813
Charles Ives	October 20, 1874
Franz Liszt	October 22, 1811
Georges Bizet	October 25, 1838

Composers' Birthdays–Celebrate!

Domenico Scarlatti   October 26, 1685

NOVEMBER
Aleksandr Borodin	November 12, 1833
Aaron Copland	November 14, 1900
W. C. Handy	November 16, 1873
Tommy Dorsey	November 19, 1905
Benjamin Britten	November 22, 1913
Scott Joplin	November 24, 1868

DECEMBER
Jean Sibelius	December 8, 1865
Hector Berlioz	December 11, 1803
Ludwig van Beethoven	December 17, 1770
Giacomo Puccini	December 23, 1858